B.E.T. GROUP
BUS FLEETS
THE FINAL YEARS

B.E.T. GROUP
BUS FLEETS

THE FINAL YEARS

JIM BLAKE

PEN & SWORD
TRANSPORT

Published in 2017 by
Pen & Sword Transport
an imprint of
Pen & Sword Books Ltd
47 Church Street
Barnsley
South Yorkshire
S70 2AS

Copyright © James Blake, 2017

ISBN 9 781 47385 726 1

Typeset by Matthew Wharmby
Printed and bound in China by Imago Publishing Limited

Pen & Sword Books Ltd incorporates the imprints of Pen & Sword Archaeology, Atlas, Aviation,
Battleground, Discovery, Family History, History, Maritime, Military, Naval, Politics, Railways,
Select, Transport, True Crime, and Fiction, Frontline Books, Leo Cooper, Praetorian Press,
Seaforth Publishing and Wharncliffe.

For a complete list of Pen & Sword titles please contact
PEN & SWORD BOOKS LIMITED
47 Church Street, Barnsley, South Yorkshire, S70 2AS, England
E-mail: enquiries@pen-and-sword.co.uk
Website: www.pen-and-sword.co.uk

CONTENTS

ABOUT THE AUTHOR

I was born at the end of 1947, just five days before the 'Big Four' railway companies, and many bus companies – including London Transport – were nationalised by Clement Attlee's Labour government.

Like most young lads born in the early post-war years, I soon developed a passionate interest in railways, the myriad steam engines still running on Britain's railways in those days in particular. However, because my home in Canonbury Avenue, Islington, was just a few minutes' walk from North London's last two tram routes, the 33 in Essex Road and the 35 in Holloway Road and Upper Street, my parents often took me on these for outings to the South Bank, particularly to the Festival of Britain which was held there in the last summer they ran, in 1951. Moreover, my father worked at the GPO's West Central District Office in Holborn and often travelled to and from work on the 35 tram. As a result, I knew many of the tram crews, who would let me stand by the driver at the front of the trams as they travelled through the Kingsway Tram Subway. This was an unforgettable experience for a four-year-old! In addition, my home was in the heart of North London's trolleybus system, with route 611 actually passing my home, and one of the busiest and most complicated trolleybus junctions in the world – Holloway, Nag's Head – a short ride away along Holloway Road. Here, the trolleybuses' overhead almost blotted out the sky! Thus from a very early age, I developed an interest in buses and trolleybuses which was equal to that of my interest in railways, and I have retained both until the present day.

I was educated at my local Highbury County Grammar School, and later at Kingsway College, by coincidence a stone's throw from the old tram subway. I was first bought a camera for my 14th birthday at the end of 1961, which was immediately put to good use photographing the last London trolleybuses in North West London on their very snowy last day a week later. Three years later, I started work as an administrator for the old London County Council at County Hall, by coincidence adjacent to the former Festival of Britain site. I travelled to and from work on bus routes 171 or 172, which had replaced the 33 and 35 trams mentioned above.

By now, my interest in buses and trolleybuses had expanded to include those of other operators, and I travelled throughout England and Wales between 1961 and 1968 in pursuit of them, being able to afford to travel further afield after starting work. I also bought a colour cine-camera in 1965, with which I was able to capture what is now very rare footage of long-lost buses, trolleybuses and steam locomotives. Where the latter are concerned, I was one of the initial purchasers of the unique British Railways 'Pacific' locomotive 71000 *Duke of Gloucester*, which was the last ever passenger express engine built for use in Britain before the end of mainline steam construction in 1960. Other preservationists laughed at our group which had purchased what, in effect, was a cannibalised hulk from Barry scrapyard at the end of 1973, but they laughed on the other side of their faces when, after extensive and innovative rebuilding, it steamed again in 1986. It has since become one of the best-known and loved preserved British locomotives, often returning to the main lines.

Although I spent thirty-five years in local government administration, with the LCC's successor, the Greater London Council, then Haringey Council and finally literally back on my old doorstep, with Islington Council, I also took a break from office drudgery in 1974/5 and actually worked on the buses as a conductor at London Transport's Clapton Garage, on local routes 22, 38 and 253. Working on the latter, a former tram and trolleybus route, in particular was an unforgettable experience. I was recommended for promotion as an inspector, but rightly thought that taking such a job with the surname Blake was unwise in view of the then-current character of the same name and occupation in the *On The Buses* TV series and films, and so declined the offer and returned to County Hall!

By this time, I had begun to have my transport photographs published in various books and magazines featuring buses. I had also started off the North London Transport Society, which catered for enthusiasts interested in the subject. In conjunction with this group, I have also compiled and published a number of books since 1977, featuring many of the 100,000 or so transport photographs I have taken over the years.

Also through the North London Transport Society, I became involved in setting up and organising various events for transport enthusiasts in 1980, notably the North Weald Bus Rally which the group took over in 1984; it has raised thousands of pounds for charity ever since. These events are still going strong today.

In addition to my interest in public transport, I also have an interest in the popular music of the late 1950s and early 1960s, in particular that of the eccentric independent record producer, songwriter and manager Joe Meek. In Joe's tiny studio above a shop in Holloway Road (not far from the famous trolleybus junction) he wrote and produced *Telstar* by The Tornados, which became the first British pop record to make No.1 in America, at the end of 1962, long before The Beatles had even been heard of over there! When Joe died in February 1967, I set up an Appreciation Society for his music, which is still going strong today. His music has a very distinctive sound.

I also enjoy a pint or two (and usually more) of real ale. I have two grown-up daughters, Margaret and Felicity, and three grandchildren, Gracie, Freddie and Oscar, at the time of writing. I still live in North London, having moved to my present home in Palmers Green in 1982.

INTRODUCTION

During the 1960s, the BET (British Electric Traction) group of bus companies operated approximately half of the inter-urban and rural bus services in England and Wales. This group was semi-nationalised, having been affiliated to the four main line railway companies prior to their absorption within British Railways in 1948. At this period, the operators within the group had a wide variety of vehicle types, encompassing virtually all chassis and body makes then to be seen in service, and were also well-known for their distinctive, traditional liveries. In addition to the bus companies, there were also some coach-only operators within the group, for example Black & White of Cheltenham who were a central part of the Associated Motorways group which ran express services throughout the country, and Timpsons of Catford, South London, who ran coastal express services. As the 1960s drew to a close, the fascinating array of vehicle types was rapidly being depleted as newer, standardised one-man-operated vehicles replaced the older ones, whilst following its acquisition by the nationalised Tilling Group (Transport Holding Company) in November 1967, the BET group became part of the National Bus Company in early 1969, and before long the operators' distinctive liveries too became just a memory.

Throughout most of the 1960s, I travelled to many of these operators and photographed their vehicles, notably on tours run by the Omnibus Touring Circle, as well as spending many summer Saturdays at London's Victoria Coach Station where their service buses, as well as express coaches, could be seen.

I was fortunate to have been able to capture much of this changing transport scene on film, and am pleased to be able to present some of my photographs in this volume. Most have never been published before.

I must put on record my thanks to the PSV Circle, from whose records most of the vehicle details included herein are taken, as well as to my old friends Paul Everett and Ken Wright, who were often with me when I took the photographs all those years ago, and have helped refresh my memory regarding some of them. Also, may I thank Colin Clarke and John Scott-Morgan for helping make this book possible!

JIM BLAKE
Palmers Green
5 April 2015

A BRIEF LOOK AT THE INDIVIDUAL OPERATORS

THE DISTRIBUTION of BET fleets around England and Wales was quite uneven with, for instance, a concentration of them in the South East, but none in East Anglia. They may be summarised area-wise as follows:

1. Greater London:
Timpson's Coaches of Catford, including subsidiary Bourne & Balmer of Croydon.*
Red Line Tours.
Samuelson's Coaches.*

2. South East:
Aldershot & District.
East Kent.
Maidstone & District, including subsidiaries Skinner's Coaches and Scout Motors of Hastings.
Southdown, including subsidiaries Buck's Coaches of Worthing and Triumph Coaches of Southsea.

3. South West:
Black & White Motorways, Cheltenham.*
Devon General, including subsidiary Grey Cars.
Greenslades Tours.

4. Midlands:
City of Oxford Motor Services.
East Midland.
Midland Red (Birmingham & Midland Motor Omnibus Company).
Potteries Motor Traction (PMT).
Stratford Blue.
Trent Motor Traction.

5. North West:
North Western.
Ribble, including subsidiaries Scout and Standerwick.

6. North East:
East Yorkshire.
Hebble.
Mexborough & Swinton.
Northern General, including subsidiaries Gateshead & District, Sunderland District, Tynemouth & District, Tyneside Omnibus and Wakefield's Motors.

Sheffield United Tours.
Yorkshire Traction.
Yorkshire Woollen District.

7. Wales:
Neath & Cardiff Luxury Coaches.
Rhondda.
South Wales.
Thomas Bros, Port Talbot.
Western Welsh.

It is noteworthy that no BET fleets were based in East Anglia or in North Wales. Operators marked * were not wholly owned by British Electric Traction who, however, had a majority shareholding in them.

During the first half of the 1960s, I spent my summer holidays at Swalecliffe, and thus came to know East Kent's buses very well. Here, on 29 July 1962, a group of pre-war Leyland Titan TD4s and TD5s with post-war Park Royal bodies await disposal at Herne Bay garage. A 1947 Dennis Lancet J3, still in original condition, is just visible on the left, too. The cars in the foreground, presumably belonging to staff there, would also be collectors' pieces today!

Also at Herne Bay garage that day, CFN 142 is one of the Park Royal-bodied Dennis Lancet J3s rebuilt with full-fronts in 1959 to enable one-man operation. It has worked coastal route 37 from Whitstable, Tankerton and Swalecliffe and I had ridden there on it. These buses survived as late as 1967 in this form.

Forward-entrance Park Royal-bodied AEC Regent Vs, like WFN 836 of the 1961 batch, replaced older double-deckers like those seen above, as well as the CJG, EFN and FFN batches throughout the 1960s. East Kent was unusual in that fleet numbers were not shown on their buses and coaches; they were known by their registration numbers. This one is seen outside Herne Bay garage on route 6, also on 29 July 1962.

More unusual in East Kent's fleet was a batch of Dennis Falcon single-deckers, whose bodies were also built by Dennis. Dating from 1950, they were used on rural services with restrictive clearances, much as London Transport's GS class was. Here, on 31 July 1962, EFN 568 loads up in Broadstairs.

By now, not many of the East Kent Dennis Lancets remained in use in original condition, but CFN 120 is one of two seen outside Ramsgate's Westwood garage after use on a works service. Note their rear entrances, with sliding doors. One of the 1961 WFN batch of Park Royal-bodied AEC Reliances used on express services to and from London brings up the rear.

East Kent's first batch of AEC Regent Vs was forty strong. They were delivered in 1959 to replace a similar number of wartime Guy Arabs still with original utility bodywork. Their Park Royal bodies were unusual in being full-fronted. One of these, PFN 865, is seen also on 31 July 1962 at Ramsgate Harbour, with all the trappings of a typical early 1960s seaside resort!

Also at Ramsgate Harbour, Catford-based BET coach operator Timpsons had their own small coach station, at which stands their HUV 444 which has worked an excursion. This elderly coach had been reinstated for the 1962 season, and was unusual in being a 1947 AEC Regal III that had originally had a half-cab body, but was rebodied in 1954 with a Duple Vega body of a type more usually seen on Bedford chassis.

Typical of East Kent double-deckers delivered in the earlier 1950s is GFN 836, one of the 1952 batch of 'tin front' Guy Arabs, with a Park Royal body equipped with platform doors. It lays over with a group of other East Kent buses in Canterbury Bus Station on 3 August 1962. The modern bus station and buildings in the background are a result of the wartime bombing of Canterbury as part of the Luftwaffe's so-called *Baedeker* raids.

The cutting down of similar 1951 Park Royal-bodied Guy Arab III FFN 380 had recently caused quite a stir when it was seen on Thursday, 9 August 1962 on the seafront at Minnis Bay, giving an idea what a London Transport RT or RTL would have looked like if so treated, since the bodywork was very similar to them. Several more were similarly treated to replace wartime utility Guy Arabs, and – ironically – hired to London Transport for their Round London Sightseeing Tour ten years later!

Midland Red (or to give it its full title, the Birmingham & Midland Motor Omnibus Company) was one of the largest BET fleets, whose operations stretched right across from Leicestershire to Worcestershire. They operated express coach services to London's Victoria Coach Station, being quick to capitalise on the opening of the M1 Motorway in 1959, for which their standard CM5T motorway coach No.4807 was meant. In common with many BMMO vehicles, it was built at the company's own workshops. It has arrived at Victoria on 26 April 1963.

Also at Victoria that day, brand new Black & White Plaxton 'Panorama'-bodied Leyland Leopard No.240 has arrived from Cheltenham Spa, the company's hometown and hub of the Associated Motorways network, within which coaches from BET and Tilling Group companies operated throughout England and Wales.

An older and more unusual Black & White coach on the same service is No.185, a Guy Arab LUF with centre-entrance Willowbrook body, dating from 1956.

BET operator
Southdown purchased Harrington bodywork for many of their coaches, built at Hove in their home territory. No.1743 is a new Harrington 'Cavalier'-bodied Leyland Leopard seating 51 passengers, also at Victoria on 26 April 1963.

A much different Southdown vehicle at Victoria on 31 May 1963 is their No.396, a wartime Park Royal-bodied utility Guy Arab dating from 1945, and later converted to open-top for seafront service. On this occasion, however, it has been in use as a grandstand at the Epsom Derby.

On the same occasion, two East Midland coaches are parked at Victoria. New Plaxton-bodied AEC Reliance No.261, which is 36ft long and seats 49, contrasts with 1960 Weymann dual-purpose bodied Leyland Tiger Cub No.253. These chassis and body makes typified BET fleets at this period.

For the 1963 season, most operators were 'getting in on the act' of buying 36ft-long coaches, following the change in legislation to allow this longer size of vehicle the previous year. North Western No.958 is a recently-delivered Leyland Leopard with splendid Alexander 49-seat bodywork, of a type then more usually seen on Scottish coaches. It is unloading passengers and luggage here.

I spent my 1963 summer holiday at Swalecliffe again, where elderly East Kent Park Royal-bodied Dennis Lancet J3 coach EFN 574 has been pressed into service on stage carriage route 41 between Whitstable and Herne Bay and loads up outside the Plough Inn. It is a matter of opinion whether the 35-seater, which looks much older than it actually was (1950), had space for all the intending passengers!

The 35-seat Lancet seen above obviously did not have sufficient seats for everyone, so 1950 Park Royal lowbridge-bodied Guy Arab III EFN 186 has also been pressed into service on busy route 41, usually the preserve of the CFN and CJG batch of Dennis Lancet J3 single-deckers at this period. It is also seen outside the Plough.

An older East Kent double-decker seen at Folkestone Bus Station on 31 July 1963 is CJG 987, an all-Leyland Titan PD2 dating from 1947. This was the only PD2 in East Kent's fleet, which followed on from a large batch of PD1s.

Of the same batch as open-topper FFN 380 seen earlier, FFN 369 is typical of the batch of Guy Arab IIIs with RT-style Park Royal bodies supplied to East Kent in 1951. It too is seen at Folkestone on 31 July 1963.

The last batch of Guy Arabs supplied to East Kent were the Mk IV variety, also with Park Royal bodywork, and they arrived in 1957. MFN 883 is one of these, also seen in Folkestone on 31 July 1963.

East Kent's first Guy Arabs were wartime utility examples, of which BJG304 has been retained for tree-lopping duties. It is accompanied by JG 7016, one of the last pre-war Leyland Titan TD4s rebodied by Park Royal after the war to remain in service. Both are seen in the yard of Herne Bay Garage on 1 August 1963.

During the 1960s, I lived a short distance from Arsenal Football Club's Highbury Stadium. On match days, nearby Drayton Park was lined with coaches bringing the away team's supporters from all parts of the country. Here, on 15 February 1964, Ribble's 1958 Burlingham Seagull-bodied Leyland Tiger Cub PSUC1/2 No.1004 is one of several that have brought Liverpool supporters for a fifth round cup tie.

Two similar Burlingham Seagull-bodied Leyland 'Tiger Cubs' seen at Victoria Coach Station on 26 March 1964 are Trent No.23 dating from 1957, and Standerwick No.10 from 1958. The latter fleet was a subsidiary of Ribble. Note the old block of flats behind them.

Seen in East Grinstead High Street on 7 April 1964, Maidstone & District DL24 is one of a small batch of lowbridge Leyland-bodied Titan PD2/12s dating from 1951. East Grinstead was a 'border town' where London Transport Country Area buses met those of BET fleets Maidstone & District and Southdown. LT was the main operator in the town, where it had a garage. Standard LT bus stops are also evident in this picture, along with one of their RF class single-deckers.

At Victoria, the garage of Samuelson Coaches, a small BET subsidiary, was also used as an overspill for the coach station across the road. On 16 May 1964, new Southdown Marshall-bodied Leyland Panther PSU3/1R No.119 parks up there after working a relief journey from the south coast.

In contrast to the previous picture, Southdown all-Leyland centre-entrance Royal Tiger coach No.1639 is one of the last of its batch to survive, and has also worked a relief.

Of the same type as the Southdown coach above, Maidstone & District CO282 dates from 1952, and has worked a service to Victoria from Leysdown holiday camp. Its days are now numbered, too.

An unusual visitor to Victoria Coach Station on 16 May 1964 is Sheffield United Tours' No.307, a 1961 AEC Reliance with 36-seat Plaxton bodywork. This operator was also a BET subsidiary. Two East Kent and one Maidstone & District coach are seen in the background.

By 27 June 1964, half-cab coaches and single-deckers were quite rare, the more so with major operators. However, 1950 Harrington-bodied AEC Regal III coach C121, of Maidstone & District subsidiary Skinner's Coaches of Hastings, has worked up to Victoria. The bodywork is very much a pre-war design, but from 1951 onwards underfloor-engined coaches with full-fronted bodywork would be the norm.

Midland Red was a pioneer of underfloor-engined buses and coaches; their Duple-bodied C2 No.3347 also dates from 1950 and is seen at Victoria the same evening. It is a touring coach with only 26 luxurious seats. Some of this batch were given new Plaxton bodies in the mid-1960s.

We were back to the Isle of Thanet again for our 1964 summer holiday! Here, on 29 July 1964, East Kent 1963 Park Royal-bodied AEC Regent V 6803 FN just manages to squeeze through Canterbury's historic Westgate.

Also in Canterbury that day, 1947 all-Leyland Titan PD1 CJG 961 is one of the last survivors of this batch, and will also be replaced by new Regent Vs.

With similar Leyland body, albeit to highbridge configuration, Maidstone & District DH418 is a Titan PD2/12 dating from 1951 and arrives at Canterbury Bus Station on route 67, which was worked jointly with East Kent.

Southdown also had Leyland-bodied Titans. No.375 dates from 1948 and was one of the last survivors of its batch of PD2s when seen at Brighton's Old Steine on 19 August 1964.

The first of many day trips I did to the Midlands in the mid-1960s was on Sunday, 14 March 1965 by train from St. Pancras to Leicester, where Midland Red Alexander-bodied Daimler Fleetline No.5284 is seen working local service L8 at the city's main bus station. Leicester had a somewhat odd arrangement, with its own City Corporation as well as Midland Red working such routes. Note the blanked off offside illuminated advert panel.

More typical of Midland Red's double-deckers at this period was 1957 D7 No.4552, built in the company's own workshops and seen here at Leicester, Southgate Street.

Derby-based BET fleet Trent Motor Traction also served Leicester. Here, their 1959 MCW-bodied Leyland Atlantean No.449 prepares to depart from the bus station for Loughborough on route 625, which was jointly worked with Midland Red. By now, rear-engined double-deckers such as the Leyland Atlantean and Daimler Fleetline were operating for many BET fleets, though rear-entrance, half-cab, front-engined double-deckers were also still being built for them. This early Atlantean has its illuminated offside advert panel still in use!

On Easter Saturday, 17 April 1965, Victoria Coach Station is in the throes of being enlarged, and the old block of flats seen in previous pictures herein demolished. And with a broom propped up against it, Ribble 1955 Burlingham Seagull-bodied Leyland Tiger Cub No.962 lays over. Two typical BTC (Tilling Group) ECW-bodied Bristol coaches are seen on the left.

Sporting events at Wembley Stadium were always a 'Mecca' for transport enthusiasts fifty or so years ago, with buses and coaches of all shapes and sizes, makes and ages bringing spectators from all around the country. On 24 April 1965, the Amateur FA Cup Final is on and 1964 City of Oxford Motor Services 53-seat Marshall-bodied AEC Reliance single-decker No.611 is being booked in to the coach park.

During the 1950s and 1960s, it was common practice for retired buses and coaches to be modified for use as breakdown tenders. Here on 30 April 1965 at Maidstone & District's Knightrider Street headquarters in Maidstone is CKO 988, originally a pre-war Leyland Tiger TS8 coach and so modified in 1964.

I also visited Maidstone & District's Medway Towns depots that day. Here at Chatham are two of their wartime Guy Arabs, rebodied in 1952 by Weymann. On the right, DH66, an Arab I dating from 1944, is still apparently in use, but on the left, 1945 Arab II DH76 is awaiting disposal, and with others of its batch has, for some reason, been painted grey.

Maidstone & District also rebodied their wartime Bristol K6As. This one, DH160, was new in 1945 and given a new Weymann body in 1951. It is seen in Gillingham Bus Station.

Park Royal 'Royalist' coach bodies were quite rare, but this 1955 AEC Reliance, PXO 974, belonging to Timpsons of Catford, carries one when seen unloading its passengers at Central Hall, Westminster on 4 May 1965.

Another AEC Reliance, this time with Plaxton bodywork, is Potteries Motor Traction C815, new in 1956 and acquired from Rowbotham of Harrishead in 1959, arrives at Wembley for the 1965 Rugby Cup Final on 8 May 1965. It was quite typical of BET fleets during the 1950s and 1960s to acquire the vehicles and operations of smaller operators in their areas.

Hebble was a small Yorkshire-based bus and coach company which was part of the BET group. Also on 8 May 1965, their very smart 1954 Bellhouse-Hartwell-bodied Leyland Royal Tiger No.35 is already a great rarity, and has also brought Rugby supporters down to London for the Rugby Cup, but instead of going to Wembley is parked up in Midland Road, between St. Pancras and the former Midland Railway Somers Town Goods Depot. This was a favourite place for coaches visiting London to be parked up in those days. Presumably, the Rugby supporters have had to make their own way to Wembley using London Transport's Metropolitan Line!

Buses and coaches on private hire work also came to Victoria Coach Station. Here, on 15 May 1965, Maidstone & District DH427, a 1954 Leyland Titan PD2/12 with standard Weymann 'Orion' bodywork based at Chatham, stands beneath the old block of flats being demolished next to the coach station.

At this time, an overtime ban by London Transport bus crews meant that private coaches had to be hired to operate their Round London Sightseeing Tour. Here, also on 15 May 1965, Samuelson's 1959 Duple-bodied AEC Reliance WLP 438, whose garage was just around the corner, does the honours when seen on the stand in Buckingham Palace Road alongside Victoria railway station. Note the large board fixed to the LT 'dolly stop'. The fare for the tour was 5/- (25p) yet a Red Rover ticket for unlimited travel throughout the Central (red bus) Area only cost a shilling more at 6/- (30p)!

Redevelopment work continues at Victoria Coach Station on 22 May 1965, as East Kent 1954 Duple-bodied Dennis Lancet LU2 HJG 12 arrives. By now, the M2 motorway has speeded up coach travel to this operator's area, as its blind shows. This type of coach was quite rare, since Dennis' underfloor-engined single-deck buses and coaches never achieved the popularity that their half-cab models did.

Despite also having Duple coachwork, Southdown coach No.1614, seen at Victoria the same day, has a different style and is a Leyland Royal Tiger dating from 1951 but now relegated to relief duties only. Both, however, have 41-seat centre-entrance bodies.

A trip to various Southdown depots on 30 May 1965 finds their 1952 all-Leyland Royal Tiger PSU1/15 No. 1626 out of use at their County Oak, Crawley depot. Somewhat unusually for this type, it had latterly been converted to 'dual purpose' mode, i.e. capable of being used as a single-deck bus as well as a coach. This explains why it has been given a larger destination blind box.

On the same day, conventional Southdown single-decker No.1539 stands at Brighton's Pool Valley Bus Station. It is a 1953 East Lancs-bodied Leyland Royal Tiger PSU1/13 with 41 seats. Its very informative blind is of note, typical of Southdown at the time!

Also at Pool Valley that day is Southdown's 1951 all-Leyland Titan PD2/12 No.716, which will soon be withdrawn.

For Derby Day 1965, 2 June 1965, East Kent wartime utility Guy Arab I BJG 354, still with original Park Royal bodywork albeit cut down in 1959 to open-top, has made it up to Victoria Coach Station and contrasts with one of the recently-delivered East Kent Park Royal-bodied AEC Reliances on the left.

Aldershot & District was another BET operator, with services in Hampshire and Surrey beyond the London Transport area. On 5 June 1965, their 1954 AEC Reliance No.251 with unusual Strachan coach bodywork is seen on hire to Southdown when queuing up to enter the coach station. During peak times, coaches had to queue all along Buckingham Palace Road, and around the corner towards Sloane Square to reach Victoria Coach Station, and often unloaded in the street! Some of this batch of Reliances were given new Weymann bus bodies in 1967.

Entering the coach station amid its rebuilding works the same day is Black & White 1952 Willowbrook-bodied Leyland Royal Tiger PSU1/13 No.151 on their busy Associated Motorways service to Cheltenham. This is its last season of service before withdrawal.

Another elderly Leyland Royal Tiger coach to be seen at Victoria Coach Station that day is Maidstone & District C272. Its odd-looking bodywork is a prototype built by Harrington in 1952; the strange-looking windscreen arrangement was not perpetuated on the later 'production' batch!

A third early Leyland Royal Tiger at Victoria Coach Station that day is Southdown No.1676, which has Harrington 41-seat bodywork. Built in 1951, it was originally a touring coach seating only 26 and numbered 1816, but was rebuilt to this configuration for use on express 'reliefs' in 1961. A sticker saying it is on 'relief' is below its nearside windscreen.

On 9 June 1965, I travelled by South Midland coach to Oxford to visit the local BET operator City of Oxford Motor Services. This fleet had a very ornate livery of maroon with what was described as 'duck egg blue' relief bands, with black lining. At the City's bus station is 1950 Weymann-bodied AEC Regent III No. H912 (the 'H' indicating a highbridge, i.e. standard 14ft 6ins height, double-decker) about to depart on trunk route 34 to Reading. At the time, it was the oldest bus in the fleet still in service.

Clearly showing the difference in height between highbridge and lowbridge double-deckers (thus named to enable them to pass beneath low railway bridges, and usually 14ft 3ins in height), 1952 Park Royal-bodied AEC Regent III No.172 has just arrived at the bus station. This batch of buses was also due for early withdrawal.

City of Oxford maintained an allegiance to AEC for many years, so bought a batch of their Bridgemasters in 1962. With Park Royal bodywork similar to that on the East Kent Regent Vs seen earlier in this book, No.324 rests at the bus station. An attempt at providing lowbridge bodies that did not have to rely on sunken side gangways on the upper deck as hitherto standard, the Bridgemaster was nowhere near as successful as the similarly configured Bristol Lodekka.

Illustrating both high- and lowbridge Weymann-bodied AEC exposed-radiator Regent Vs in the City of Oxford fleet, No.945 is a highbridge example dating from 1956, whilst No.194 beside it has lowbridge bodywork and dates from 1957.

A stranger in the camp is City of Oxford 1961 Dennis Loline II No.301, which was one of five supplied that year with East Lancs bodywork. This type of bus was also an attempt to produce a lowbridge vehicle with standard centre-gangway upper-deck seating. One of its best customers was Aldershot & District whose territory included Dennis' home town, Guildford.

City of Oxford also favoured AEC chassis for its single-deck bus and coach fleet. By now, No.736 was the company's oldest single-decker, a Reliance with Willowbrook 43-seat bodywork dating only from 1955. The standard life of a provincial bus in 1965 was usually around 12-14 years at this period.

Two more modern City of Oxford AEC Reliances at Oxford Bus Station on 9 June 1965 are Park Royal-bodied No.759 built in 1960, and Willowbrook-bodied No.794 dating from 1964. These clearly show the change of bodywork style typical of BET fleets over the four years between them.

Another BET operator to serve Oxford was Stratford Blue, whose 1963 Willowbrook-bodied 'tin-front' Leyland Titan PD3/4 No.2 arrives at the bus station on route 44 from its hometown, Stratford-upon-Avon.

A last look at the City of Oxford fleet on 9 June 1965 as well-loaded 1954 Park Royal-bodied AEC Regent III No.H930 is seen with some of its fellows in the City Centre.

Greenslades Tours of Exeter was a BET group company, and here at Victoria on 19 June 1965 their 1953 Willowbrook-bodied AEC Regal IV NUO 691 has worked up to London on hire to Royal Blue on an Associated Motorways service. The coach had been new to fellow BET company Devon General.

On the same occasion, Southdown Duple-bodied Leyland Royal Tiger PSU1/15 No.1649 also dates from 1953 and was one of a batch of only five with this style of bodywork.

Victoria Coach Station's new offices flanking Buckingham Palace Road take shape beside Potteries C858, a 1958 Willowbrook-bodied Leyland Tiger Cub PSUC/1/2 acquired by them from Dawson of Ash Bank in 1960. Its bodywork was identical to that carried by a batch of AEC Reliance coaches delivered new to Potteries, also in 1958.

At Gravesend's Overcliff terminus, Southdown No.811, an East Lancs-bodied Leyland Titan PD2/12 new in 1956, is a long way from home when working route 122, which was jointly operated between Southdown and Maidstone & District, running all the way from Gravesend to Brighton, via Tonbridge, Tunbridge Wells, Crowborough and Uckfield.

A typical summer Saturday at Victoria, 3 July 1965, finds Grey Cars 1957 Beadle-Commer integral coach TCC 847 heading a queue of coaches lined up in Buckingham Palace Road waiting to get into Victoria Coach Station. Grey Cars was the coaching arm of BET fleet Devon General, and this coach is on hire to Royal Blue on one of their Associated Motorways services from the West Country. Several BET operators had coaches of this type, with Commer engines and running units built integrally into bodies produced at Beadle's Chatham factory, in similar fashion to London's Routemasters with their Park Royal bodies and AEC or Leyland mechanical parts in the 1950s.

Sunday, 4 July 1965 was the first of many day trips I made to the Birmingham area courtesy of an excursion train which ran from Paddington to Snow Hill, for the princely sum of thirty bob (£1.50) day return. On that occasion, Midland Red No.4037, one of a batch of all-Leyland Titan PD2/20s supplied to them in 1953, stands outside their Digbeth garage. Classified class LD8 by the company, these were delivered at a time when most of Midland Red's buses and coaches were built by the company itself.

Back in London, a very unusual visitor caught at Parliament Square is this 1957 Burlingham Seagull-bodied Leyland Tiger Cub coach, No.101 in the fleet of small south Yorkshire BET company Mexborough & Swinton. It appears to be working a school outing.

Back to 'East Kent land' again for my 1965 summer holiday – for the last time! On 26 July 1965, rebuilt 1948 Park Royal-bodied Dennis Lancet J3 CFN 152 calls at the Old Barn in Chestfield Village, on the infrequent route 5 from Canterbury to Whitstable.

Another Dennis Lancet, 1950 Park Royal-bodied coach EFN 587 is seen at East Kent's Canterbury headquarters adapted for use as a snowplough. Presumably it was only used as such in the winter, not when this picture was taken on 28 July 1965!

Much more drastic is the conversion of former wartime Park Royal utility-bodied Guy Arab I BJG 421 to a towing wagon and breakdown tender; in fact only the registration number identifies it as once having been a double-deck bus.

At Canterbury Bus Station the same day, East Kent 1955 Weymann dual-purpose-bodied AEC Reliance KFN 215 works the long route 2 to Hastings via Ashford, which was jointly operated with fellow BET company Maidstone & District. One of East Kent's many Park Royal-bodied AEC Regent Vs brings up the rear.

Heading a group of East Kent buses in Canterbury Bus Station, 1947 all-Leyland Titan PD1 CJG 980 is one of the oldest buses in the fleet and is seen working a rush hour relief duty on local route 1. Also seen are one of the rebuilt Dennis Lancet single-deckers and a 1950 Park Royal-bodied Guy Arab.

At Herne Bay garage next day, 29 July 1965, East Kent GFN 259 is a Beadle-bodied coach, integrally constructed with running units from a pre-war Leyland Titan TD5 double-decker in 1953. In common with several other touring coaches in the fleet, it is fitted with a boat rack.

A visitor to Herne Bay that day is Timpson of Catford's 1961 Duple 'Super Vega'-bodied Thames Trader touring coach 526 BGW.

A day trip to Ramsgate on 2 August 1965 finds East Kent 1950 Park Royal lowbridge-bodied Guy Arab EFN 209 parked up by the harbour, whilst working route 65 from Deal garage. One of the company's many AEC Regent Vs is seen in the distance.

A day trip to Folkestone on 3 August 1965 finds East Kent AFN 780B, one of the 1964 batch of Park Royal-bodied AEC Regent Vs, working route 90 to Dover. Buses of this type were delivered in 1961, 1962, 1963, 1964, 1966 and 1967.

In complete contrast, also at Folkestone Bus Station, brand new Marshall-bodied 51-seat AEC Reliance DJG 357C is one of the first batch of East Kent's 36ft one-man-operated single-deckers. These replaced some of the CJG batch of Leyland PD1 double-deckers in 1965, rather than more AEC Regent Vs as had been delivered in the previous four years. However, further batches of these Regents were delivered to East Kent in 1966 and 1967, the latter being some of the last of this type built.

Representing the older generation of East Kent buses, 1947 all-Leyland Titan PD1 CJG987 and 1948 rebuilt Park Royal-bodied Dennis Lancet J3 CFN 130 are parked at East Kent's Cheriton garage the same day. This view of the Lancet shows clearly how, as well as being rebuilt with a full front, its entrance was moved from the rear to the front to allow one-man operation.

An even older survivor still on East Kent's books is 1938 Park Royal-bodied Leyland Tiger TS7 coach JG 9938, which has been in use for several years as a mobile booking office for East Kent tours at Folkestone Harbour. The notice tells how a day tour across the Channel to France costs £3 12s 6d (£3.62)! It is interesting to reflect that the style of this old coach's original 1938 body is little different from that of the 1950-built EFN Lancet coaches seen earlier. Fortunately, this splendid old vehicle survived and is smartly preserved in original condition today.

Somewhat fittingly, the last photograph I ever took of an East Kent bus when on holiday at Swalecliffe was this one of 1952 Park Royal 'tin-front'-bodied Guy Arab IV GFN 919 at the Swalecliffe, Goodwin Avenue terminus of busy route 4 to Canterbury via Whitstable. By coincidence, the first bus photograph I ever took was of a brand new AEC Regent V at this same spot back in July 1961! These were still the 4's usual allocation four years later. This Guy is unusually working an evening rush hour relief on the route.

On a day trip to Coventry on 15 August 1965, I encountered Black & White 1952 Willowbrook-bodied Leyland Royal Tiger PSU1/11 coach No.154 at the City's Pool Meadow Bus Station. It is working the Associated Motorways Cheltenham-Nottingham express service, and will be withdrawn after the 1965 season. This view nicely shows its centre entrance.

Also at Pool Meadow that day, Midland Red LD8 class all-Leyland Titan PD2/12 No.4068 works their express route X90 to Stratford-upon-Avon via Warwick. It is one of many buses of this type based at Leamington Spa.

Back in London again, Maidstone & District 1955 Harrington-bodied AEC Reliance C332 is parked up at Lincoln's Inn Fields on the evening of 18 September 1965, probably having brought a group of theatregoers up to town from Kent.

As mentioned earlier, Aldershot & District had a large fleet of Dennis Lolines. Here on 9 October 1965 their No.345, a 1958 Loline I with East Lancs bodywork, accompanies No.145, a 1948 Dennis Lance K3, also with an East Lancs body, at Camberley Station.

An oddity at Victoria Coach Station on 2 October 1965 is Southdown 1955 Harrington-bodied Leyland Royal Tiger PSU1/11 No.1832, in the light blue livery of their subsidiary, Bucks Coaches of Worthing. Despite its size, the coach has only 26 seats, being meant for luxury touring, but has been pressed into service here on one of Southdown's coastal express routes.

Seen at Newbury Bus Station on 26 March 1966, City of Oxford 1965 Weymann 49-seat dual-purpose bodied AEC Reliance No.617 typifies single-deckers being supplied to BET fleets at this time.

At Midland Red's Bearwood garage on 10 April 1966, their 'home-made' class S13 single-decker No.3949 typifies those built by this operator in the early/mid-1950s. These vehicles were now being withdrawn.

Southdown's famous full-fronted Leyland Titan PD3 open-toppers were actually 'convertible', meaning they had detachable tops for use in cold or inclement weather. For some reason, they appear not to have been photographed often bearing these, but on 30 April 1966 this one, 1963 Northern Counties-bodied PD3A No.413, does have its top fitted when arriving at Wembley for the Schoolboys' International football cup final.

London Transport's Gillingham Street garage at Victoria was used for long-distance coaches serving the nearby coach station, which in this period travelled overnight, to lay over during the day whilst their drivers had a well-earned rest in one of the many 'bed and breakfast' guest houses in the area. This view shows Yorkshire Traction 1957 Burlingham Seagull-bodied Leyland Tiger Cub PSUC1/2 No.1074, which has been working to Barnsley via their Midland Route when seen in the company of brand new Eastern Scottish Alexander-bodied Bristol RELH XA170A working their Edinburgh service on 7 May 1966. This Scottish operator was part of the nationalised Scottish Bus Group.

One of several hundred buses and coaches at Wembley on 14 May 1966 for the 1966 FA Cup Final, Ribble 1956 Tiger Cub No.963 is similar to the Yorkshire Traction example seen above. The passengers on the Ribble coach must have been pleased with the result of the match, in which Everton beat Sheffield Wednesday 3-2.

Illustrating how popular Burlingham Seagull bodywork was with BET fleets, yet another is Timpson's TGJ 479, an AEC Reliance dating from 1957. All of its batch had been withdrawn at the end of the 1965 season, but for some reason this one was reinstated. It had been at Wembley on 21 May 1966 for the Rugby Cup Final, and is seen that evening parked up at Russell Square. The reason for this is that supporters attending events at Wembley were often taken to hotels in this area after the match, enabling them to sample London's theatres or night life between match and bed!

Harrington of Hove produced some of the most striking coach bodies in the 1950s and 1960s, but sadly ceased production in the spring of 1966. One of the last bodies built by them was this 'Grenadier', fitted to brand new Grey Cars AEC Reliance No.30, seen at Wembley also on 21 May 1966. My own favourite coach body designs were this type, along with Harrington's similar 'Cavalier' and 'Crusader' types, and the Burlingham 'Seagull'.

Another new BET vehicle at Wembley that day is Ribble Marshall dual-purpose 49-seat Leyland Leopard PSU3/4R No.826. A Stevenage Travel Duple-bodied Bedford twin-steer VAL and a Harrington 'Crusader' bodied-coach behind it complete the picture. Are the two young lads behind the Leopard coach spotters?

Another of many 'northerners' at Wembley that day is 1959 Plaxton-bodied AEC Reliance No.11 in the small Yorkshire fleet of Hebble. A more modern Plaxton-bodied coach stands to the right.

Arriving at Wembley on 21 May 1966 is Maidstone & District's famous 'Knightrider' luxury coach LC1, a Harrington-bodied Commer Avenger dating from 1951. It seated only sixteen passengers, and was equipped with tables and a cocktail cabinet! Instead of their usual cream and green coach livery, it was dark blue.

London-based Red Line Tours was one of the smallest BET operators. Their 1954 Plaxton-bodied AEC Reliance OLX 3 is at Wembley on the same occasion.

Thanks to the introduction of fast electric train services to Liverpool and Manchester, I was able to make several day or weekend trips to that area during 1966 and 1967. On the first of these on Sunday, 29 May 1966 I encountered this very strange-looking single-decker at Manchester's Piccadilly Bus Station. It is North Western No.131, a Bedford VAL14 twin-steerer with Strachans bodywork. A Dennis Loline with the same operator stands behind it as one of Manchester City Transport's Leyland Atlanteans or Fleetlines passes by.

City of Oxford 1965 Park Royal-bodied AEC Renown No.351 stands at Aylesbury Bus Station, one of few places where this operator's buses could be seen in service alongside those of London Transport, on 4 June 1966.

Of the same batch as the one above, City of Oxford's Renown No.353 is an odd man out amongst all the ECW-bodied Bristols in the Tilling green or cream and green livery of United Counties when seen laying over in Bedford Bus Station on 19 June 1966.

This scene at Victoria Coach Station on 25 June 1966 nicely shows the new offices added to the original 1930s buildings in 1965. In the foreground is Southdown No.1000, first of a large batch of Beadle-bodied Leyland Tiger Cub coaches delivered in 1954, and now nearing withdrawal.

On the same occasion, HFN 2 is a Duple-bodied Leyland Royal Tiger new to East Kent in 1953, primarily for touring work. Southdown also had a batch of similar coaches.

A trip to Nottingham on 26 June 1966 finds North Western 1957 Burlingham Seagull-bodied Leyland Tiger Cub PSUC1/2 No.704 working their express service 2 to Manchester in Huntingdon Street Bus Station. This coach was withdrawn at the end of the 1966 season.

At fellow BET operator Trent Motor Traction's Nottingham Depot the same day, 1957 MCW Orion-bodied Leyland Titan PD2/12 No.777 accompanies 1954 Willowbrook dual-purpose-bodied Leyland Tiger Cub PSUC1/2T No.120. The latter was the last of its batch to remain in service at this time.

1953 Southdown Duple-bodied Leyland Royal Tiger PSU1/16 No.1840 still looks smart when arriving at Victoria Coach Station on relief duty on 2 July 1966.

On the same occasion, Trent 1956 Willowbrook dual-purpose-bodied Leyland Tiger Cub PSUC1/2T No.44 has worked up to London on hire to United Counties, one of whose dual-purpose Bristol MW/ECW vehicles stands behind it.

Under the trolleybus wires in Derby on 3 July 1966, Potteries Motor Transport 1959 Leyland Atlantean No.L9775 is an early example with Weymann lowbridge bodywork. It is seen on route 90 from Derby to Longton, worked jointly with fellow BET operator Trent.

On the evening of 15 July 1966, Southdown 1956 Beadle-Commer TS3 integral touring coach No.2 waits at the traffic lights at the western end of Victoria Embankment, outside Westminster Station.

I visited Manchester again on 16 July 1966. In the city's Lower Mosley Street bus and coach station (which takes its name from the well-known family that included Sir Oswald Mosley), North Western 1954 Weymann 44-seat AEC Reliance No.558 is working a limited stop, cross-Pennine service to Barnsley.

A most unlikely vehicle to be seen at Cheltenham Coach Station on 24 July 1966 is Sunderland District Burlingham-bodied Leyland Tiger Cub No.321 dating from 1961. This operator was one of several subsidiary fleets of major BET company Northern General.

This view nicely shows Black & White Motorways' Cheltenham Coach Station, hub of the Associated Motorways network, with their 1954 Duple-bodied Guy Arab LUF No.172 in the foreground.

Also a Guy Arab LUF, of which Black & White had several, No.189 has Willowbrook bodywork and dates from 1956. The boards either side of it, showing the many destinations served by Associated Motorways, are of note. Cheltenham was an important interchange point for express services from across the country until the spread of motorways rendered the coach station redundant.

I was back in the north-west again on 6 August 1966, this time visiting Stockport. This was the home town of BET operator North Western, whose 1955 Weymann-bodied Leyland Tiger Cub PSUC1/2 No.582 stands outside their main garage.

Elderly 1949 North Western all-Leyland lowbridge Titan PD2/1 No.250 contrasts with one of their more recent rear-engined double-deckers, an Alexander-bodied Daimler Fleetline, when seen in Stockport Bus Station.

Of the same vintage, Titan PD2/1 No. 258 has a lowbridge Weymann body. A group of other North Western buses may be seen in the background.

In contrast to the older Leyland Titans seen above, North Western's 1965 Alexander-bodied Daimler Fleetline No.189 has been fitted experimentally with a Cummins engine, giving it a larger bustle at the rear. It was redesignated type CRC6 as a result.

In a very sorry state after a serious accident in which it struck a tree, North Western 1958 dual-purpose Willowbrook-bodied AEC Reliance No.755 stands outside the company's central works. It had to be rebodied as a result.

Also at North Western's works, 1948 all-Leyland lowbridge Titan PD2/1 No.224 has met a fate that often befalls withdrawn buses – relegation to driver training duties.

Very similar to the North Western examples seen earlier, East Midland 44-seat Willowbrook-bodied Leyland Tiger Cub R372 dates from 1958, and is seen in Chesterfield Bus Station on 14 August 1966.

Mexborough & Swinton was one of the smaller BET fleets, serving the area around those two South Yorkshire towns. At their depot, also on 14 August 1966, is their No.54, a Weymann-bodied Leyland Tiger Cub PSUC1/1, new in 1959.

At this period, Mexborough & Swinton had suffered from a shortage of buses, and acquired a number of early post-war Leyland Titans from fellow BET operator Southdown. This one, now their No.20, is an all-Leyland PD2/1 dating from 1948, also seen at their Rawmarsh depot. It is interesting that its front blind box has been altered to meet the requirements of its new operator.

Less exotic is Mexborough & Swinton's 1960 Weymann lowbridge-bodied Leyland Atlantean No.3, seen changing crew outside Rawmarsh depot en route for Rotherham. This was one of a batch built to replace the operator's trolleybuses, which shared their wires with those of Rotherham Corporation.

My trip to the East Midlands and South Yorkshire on 14 August 1966 was one of many I attended in those days organised by the Omnibus Touring Circle. Our means of travel was Timpson of Catford's 1963 Plaxton Panorama-bodied AEC Reliance 552 GXX, seen at Rotherham Corporation's depot.

The last summer holiday I spent with my parents was in Hastings for the two weeks either side of the 1966 August Bank Holiday weekend. The town's main operator was Maidstone & District, whose 1959 Weymann lowbridge-bodied Leyland Atlantean DL50 is seen here heading for Bexhill on 21 August 1966. By coincidence, it not only looks very similar to the Mexborough & Swinton example seen above, but also it was delivered to replace the trolleybuses of the former Hastings Tramways system.

Some of the most unusual vehicles with any BET fleet at this period were three 1946 AEC Regal 1s with Beadle bodywork which were cut down to open-top in 1956 for operation on Hastings' 'Round the Town' tours. With Hastings Castle above it, Maidstone & District OR1 stands at the tour's Fishmarket terminus, also on 21 August 1966.

On the same day, Maidstone & District breakdown crane No.862 accompanies an Atlantean in their Hastings Depot. It has been converted from an AEC Regal coach new in 1938.

East Kent also worked into Hastings. This is their 1955 Weymann dual-purpose-bodied AEC Reliance KFN 217 based at Rye, seen at the Hastings, Warrior Square terminus of route 128 on 21 August 1966.

Hastings provided an ideal base from which to travel north to Maidstone & District territory, east to that of East Kent and west to that of Southdown! On 22 August 1966 I did the latter, visiting Brighton. At Pool Valley Bus Station, working the long coastal route 9, Southdown 1965 Northern Counties-bodied Leyland PD3/4 No.257 looks almost like an Atlantean thanks to having an experimental frontal design. It accompanies No.557, a Guy Arab IV with Park Royal bodywork dating from 1956.

Also at Pool Valley, Southdown No.1519 is an East Lancs-bodied Leyland Royal Tiger PSUI/13 single-decker dating from 1953. It is on route 36 bound for East Grinstead, where it will meet London Transport Green Line route 708 running all the way to Hemel Hempstead!

Around the corner in Old Steine, Southdown 1948 all-Leyland Titan PD2/1 No.388 works an evening rush hour turn on local route 49A. At this period, such services were pooled between Southdown, Brighton Corporation and Tilling Group fleet Brighton, Hove & District. This Titan is of the same batch as the one seen above with Mexborough & Swinton.

Back in Hastings on 23 August 1966, Maidstone & District 1954 Leyland Titan PD2/12 DH421 carries typical Weymann Orion bodywork and accompanies one of the company's subsidiary Skinner's Coaches Harrington 'Wayfarer'-bodied AEC Reliance coaches at Hastings Cricket Ground.

At the same location, Maidstone & District C318 also dates from 1954, and is an AEC Reliance with Harrington centre-entrance 37-seat bodywork which has been on a day tour around the historic town.

On 23 August 1966, I travelled north to visit Maidstone & District territory, wherein we see their DH128 outside Tunbridge Wells Station. This was a 1944 utility Bristol K6A rebodied by Weymann in 1951. Several operators throughout the country rebodied their wartime buses in the early/mid-1950s, but by 1966 most had been withdrawn. However, several remained in use with M&D.

M&D's all-Leyland Titan PD2/12 DH396 was new in 1951, and this type were still the mainstay of long route 119, jointly worked with Southdown and running from Tunbridge Wells to Brighton. It too is seen in Tunbridge Wells.

The combination of a lowbridge body, built by Park Royal, and 8ft width gives Maidstone & District AEC Regent V DL35, the first of its batch dating from 1956, a rather squat appearance. It too is seen in Tunbridge Wells on 23 August 1966.

From Tunbridge Wells, I travelled on to Maidstone, at whose Knightrider Street Bus Station stands Maidstone & District DH471. This Weymann-bodied Guy Arab IV had been ordered by Chatham & District before M&D took them over, and dates from 1955.

Typical of Maidstone & District single-deckers at this period is S254, an AEC Reliance with Harrington 42-seat bodywork built in 1958. It arrives at Knightrider Street Bus Station under the watchful eye of one of the company's inspectors.

I continued beyond Maidstone to Chatham, where earlier M&D single-decker S219, a 1956-built AEC Reliance with Willowbrook 42-seat bodywork, lays over after working a relief duty on route 144.

At the company's Chatham, Luton garage, two rebodied wartime Bristol K6As await disposal. Nearest the camera, DH124 was rebodied with a Weymann Orion body in 1954, whilst DH151 has an earlier example from the same manufacturer fitted in 1951.

On 24 August 1966, I travelled across to Eastbourne, where Southdown 1955 Park Royal-bodied Guy Arab IV No.543 stands outside the bus station whilst working a relief on their route 191.

On the same day, I then travelled to Uckfield using the Southern Region branch from Lewes, which would be closed in January 1969 and is presently proposed to be reopened as a relief main line to Brighton. Here at the town's small bus station, Southdown 1953 East Lancs-bodied Leyland Royal Tiger PSU1/13 No.1515 has terminated on route 32.

The double-decker just visible behind the single-decker in the previous picture is Southdown 1956 East Lancs-bodied Leyland Titan PD2/12 No.807. It is changing crew outside Southdown's small Uckfield garage whilst working the long route 122 from Gravesend to Brighton.

Maidstone & District all-Leyland PD2/12 DH406 dating from 1951 stands at the same spot on another long route serving Brighton – the 119 from Tunbridge Wells. Both routes were worked jointly between Southdown and Maidstone & District.

I then continued further into Maidstone & District territory to Tunbridge Wells again, where 1944 Bristol K6A DH149 with 1954 Weymann Orion bodywork is still going strong when seen outside its garage.

In contrast at the same garage we find M&D's S312, a 30-seat Harrington-bodied Albion Nimbus dating from 1960. Several of these were based here for use on lightly used rural services or those with restricted clearances that larger buses could not negotiate.

Showing an offside view of one of the same batch, Maidstone & District Nimbus S316 is parked up at Hastings Cricket Ground on 25 August 1966.

Also on 25 August 1966, I travelled further west into Southdown territory, and here outside their Worthing garage are two of the older vehicles in their fleet – 1948 all-Leyland PD2/1 double-decker No.379 and 1951 Duple-bodied Leyland Royal Tiger PSU1/15 coach No.1805.

On the seafront at Worthing, brand new Southdown Northern Counties-bodied Leyland Titan PD3/4 No.312 gleams in the sun as it works the long coastal route 31 from Brighton to Littlehampton.

Further along the coast at Chichester, Southdown 1952 East Lancs-bodied Leyland Royal Tiger PSU1/12 No.1502 lays over at the Bus Station.

A somewhat newer Southdown single-decker at Chichester Bus Station on the same occasion is No.634, a Leyland Tiger Cub PSUC1/1 dating from 1953 and fitted with Duple Midland 39-seat bodywork.

The vehicle glimpsed next to Southdown 634 (above) is Aldershot & District 1961 Weymann-bodied AEC Reliance No.388, working the summer-only limited stop service 19A from Aldershot to Bognor Regis. By coincidence, the single-decker next to it is Southdown 633, of the same batch as the one seen above.

Back at Hastings the same evening (25 August 1966) an oddity to be seen at the Cricket Ground is Maidstone & District's subsidiary Skinner's Coaches 1952 AEC Regal IV C122 with rare Gurney Nutting 37-seat coachwork.

Possibly the most bizarre day trip I ever undertook in the 1960s was when on 27 August 1966 I travelled by train from Hastings to Tonbridge, then bought a 6/- Green Rover ticket on London Transport's route 403 and travelled all the way across to Guildford and Woking via Croydon and Leatherhead! Here in Aldershot & District's Guildford garage is a splendid 1950 Strachans-bodied Dennis Lancet J3, complete with rear entrance. Several of these ancient-looking single-deckers still survived in this area at the time.

Aldershot & District had many Dennis buses and coaches owing to that firm's chassis-building factory being in Guildford. This is their No.241, a Falcon PS, also with Strachans bodywork, dating from 1954 and seen in their Woking garage.

When Dennis stopped building single-deck bus chassis, Aldershot & District turned to AEC. Here outside Woking garage is their 1957 Reliance No.307, which carries Weymann bodywork.

Dennis still, however, continued to produce double-deck bus chassis well into the 1960s, in the shape of the Loline. These were the mainstay of A&D's fleet, of which No.459 has Alexander bodywork and is a Loline III dating from 1962, seen also at Woking.

One of Maidstone & District's last two 1952 all-Leyland Royal Tiger coaches, C286, is seen at Winchelsea Church on a tour on August Bank Holiday Monday, 29 August 1966.

The tour also took us to Rye, where East Kent 1950 Park Royal lowbridge-bodied Guy Arab III EFN 201 is seen outside the railway station. These buses were now being withdrawn.

Next day, 30 August 1966, I travelled further eastwards into East Kent territory. Here at their Ashford garage, 1948 Dennis Lancet J3 CFN 134 with rebuilt Park Royal bodywork is delicensed awaiting disposal.

Also at Ashford garage, 1950 lowbridge Park Royal-bodied Guy Arab III EFN 182 makes an interesting comparison with FFN 393, with the same chassis and body make dating from 1951 but with highbridge bodywork similar to that on London's RTs.

Two more East Kent Guy Arabs compared. In Folkestone Bus Station are FFN 390 of the 1951 batch, and GFN 918, a Guy Arab IV with similar Park Royal bodywork but a 'tin front', built in 1952.

East Kent 1951 Park Royal-bodied Leyland Royal Tiger PSU1/15 FFN 448, complete with boat racks, is working a day excursion when seen in Folkestone Bus Station.

Also at Folkestone on 30 August 1966 is brand new East Kent Park Royal-bodied AEC Regent V GJG 759D, which I rode on to Dover! Yet another batch of these buses was supplied to East Kent in 1967, some of the last AEC Regents built.

At East Kent's Dover garage, 1950 Dennis-bodied Falcon P3 EFN 569 is by now due for early withdrawal.

So also is 1950 lowbridge Park Royal-bodied Guy Arab III EFN 207, seen on Deal local route 84.

The last picture taken on my 1966 summer holiday to Hastings was of Maidstone & District 1961 Harrington Wayfarer-bodied AEC Reliance C444, now the only vehicle in the red and cream livery of their subsidiary, Scout Coaches. It is seen in Hastings on 31 August 1966 setting down passengers after operating a day tour.

On 4 September 1966, I again travelled to the north-west, this time to Liverpool. The main BET operator serving the city was Preston-based Ribble, whose 1954 Burlingham Seagull-bodied Leyland Royal Tiger PSU1/16 No.943 is seen outside their Liverpool garage after working one of their express services.

Typical of Ribble double-deckers used on stage carriage services in the area is their 1955 Weymann Orion-bodied Leyland Titan PD2/13 No.1388, seen at the garage itself. Note the unusual shape of the blind-box, which was a feature of Ribble's double-deckers.

In the depths of Ribble's Preston garage on 9 October 1966, their No.405 is an all-Leyland Royal Tiger PSU1/13 dating from 1952, and by now one of the last of these remaining in service in their fleet.

A visit to Maidstone & District's Tonbridge garage on a gloomy Saturday, 19 November 1966 finds their 1963 Northern Counties lowbridge-bodied Daimler Fleetline DL88 parked outside.

1967 was the last year in which the BET fleets remained within a separate group from the fully nationalised Tilling fleets. By then, Maidstone & District 1945 Bristol K6A DH118 was one of the oldest vehicles in service with any BET operator but was still going strong when seen at M&D's Maidstone, Knightrider Street garage on 15 March 1967. In common with others of this type, it was rebodied with a typical Weymann Orion body in 1954.

Four BET fleets provided inter-urban bus services in South Wales: Rhondda, South Wales, Thomas Brothers of Port Talbot and Western Welsh. Belonging to the latter fleet, No.599 is an oddity, being one of four Park Royal-bodied AEC Reliances built in 1955 for Green of Haverfordwest, who were taken over by Western Welsh in January 1957. It is seen at their Barry garage on 26 March 1967. Bizarrely, in more recent years this garage has been used to store steam engines which once resided in the nearby scrapyard! Today, preserved buses are kept there.

Seen under Cardiff City's trolleybus wires approaching Cardiff General Station on 26 March 1967, Western Welsh No.665 is a Park Royal-bodied AEC Regent V dating from 1956.

Ribble 1965 53-seat Marshall Leyland Leopard PSU3/1R No.584 arrives at Wembley Stadium for the 1967 Rugby Cup Final on 15 April 1967.

Seen in Southdown's Brighton Freshfield Road garage on 7 May 1967 is their 1956 Beadle-bodied Leyland Tiger Cub PSUC1/2 coach No.1071. As well as other Southdown vehicles, an Aldershot & District Park Royal-bodied AEC Reliance coach is also visible.

At Brighton's Pool Valley Bus Station the same day, two generations of Southdown Leyland Titan double-deckers are seen: 1952 all-Leyland PD2/12 No.754 (the intended subject of the photograph originally) contrasts with 1966 'Queen Mary' Northern Counties-bodied PD3/4 No.295. Both, of course, are now only a memory nearly fifty years later!

Also at Pool Valley, No.348 is one of the latest in Southdown's fleet and has recently entered service. It has a new style of Northern Counties full-fronted bodywork fitted to Leyland PD3/4 chassis and looks nowhere near as attractive as previous batches when compared with the example in the previous picture. It is about to work the long coastal route 31 from Brighton to Southsea.

Just around the corner in Old Steine, Maidstone & District 1951 all-Leyland PD2/12 DH391 arrives on the long 119 route that was jointly worked with Southdown. It passes one of their touring coaches, whilst three Brighton, Hove & District ECW-bodied Bristols are seen behind. This fleet will be amalgamated with Southdown in 1968.

Seen laying over at Bristol Omnibus's Lawrence Hill garage on 14 May 1967, Southdown 1957 Beadle-bodied Leyland Tiger Cub PSUC1/2 coach T1098 is one of eight of its batch in the blue and white livery of their subsidiary, Triumph Coaches of Southsea.

Seen outside their garage on a very wet 21 May 1967 are Sheffield United Tours Plaxton-bodied AEC Reliances Nos 290, 300 and 309. These were new in 1958, 1959 and 1960 respectively.

A very unusual visitor to Victoria Coach Station on 27 May 1967 is Northern General Weymann 'Fanfare'-bodied Guy Arab LUF 6HLW coach No.689, one of ten delivered to them in 1955. It is working a Whitsun weekend relief for fellow Tyneside operator United Automobile Services. More mundane is the Maidstone & District dual-purpose AEC Reliance following.

Still going strong on Derby Day, 7 June 1967, East Kent wartime utility Park Royal-bodied Guy Arab open-topper BJG353 gives racegoers a London sightseeing trip when seen at Westminster Station in the evening.

Southdown touring coach No.21 is a visitor to Basingstoke when seen parked there on 10 June 1967. It is a Commer TS3 with integrally constructed Beadle 'Rochester' bodywork, new in 1957.

An OTC trip to operators in the Nottingham area finds East Midland 1956 MCCW-bodied Leyland Tiger Cub PSUC1/1 R352 outside their Mansfield garage on 11 June 1967.

At the same location, their 1956 MCCW Orion-bodied, tin-front Leyland PD2/20 D116 displays a rather drab dark red livery with a cream waistband. That on the Trent Titan seen inside the garage is more attractive, with a lighter red and more cream relief.

Reflecting how times were changing in 1967, when Harold Wilson's Labour government had permitted Bristol and ECW to supply vehicles to non-Tilling Group companies, East Midland O512 is a brand new ECW-bodied Bristol RELL6G single-decker, being proudly displayed to members of the OTC!

A week later, I was back in the Midlands, this time visiting operators in the Staffordshire area. Here at Potteries Motor Traction's Hanley garage is 1958 Northern Counties-bodied 69-seat Daimler CVD6-30 H8900.

A more recent Potteries Daimler seen on the same occasion is H992, a Northern Counties-bodied 76-seat Fleetline CR6LX. It was new in October 1962 to Beckett & Sons of Bucknall, whose business was acquired by Potteries in March 1963. Note the nasty dent on its front nearside upper deck window pillar.

Potteries had a very varied fleet, both with chassis and body makes, partly because the company had taken over several small independent operators in the Stoke-on-Trent area. Single-deckers S678, a 1956 Burlingham-bodied AEC Reliance, and S509, a 1955 Willowbrook-bodied Leyland Tiger Cub PSUC1/1, also at Hanley, illustrate the point. Both were acquired with the firm Baxter of Hanley in December 1958.

Potteries SN8759 is a more recent single-decker in their fleet, seen amid a good variety of other buses based at Hanley. It is a Willowbrook-bodied Albion Aberdonian new to Potteries in 1958 and something of a rarity in a BET fleet.

An older Daimler double-decker at Hanley that day is L6663, a CVG5 with lowbridge Northern Counties bodywork new in 1956.

Single-decker SN926 represents more modern single-deckers in Potteries' fleet, and is also more akin to those in other BET fleets. It is a Leyland Leopard PSU3/3R with Willowbrook 54-seat bodywork new in 1962.

Next on the agenda on 18 June 1967 was a visit to Potteries' Stoke-on-Trent garage, where their L679 is posed for us. This was also acquired from Baxter of Hanley and is a Willowbrook lowbridge-bodied Leyland Titan PD2/20 new in 1957.

Smart Weymann Fanfare-bodied AEC Reliance coach SN5616 stands behind it. It was new in 1955.

One of Potteries' oldest double-deckers at this time was 1947 Northern Counties lowbridge-bodied Leyland Titan PD2/1 L337, seen at their Stoke-on-Trent garage.

Potteries L466 is also seen at Stoke. It was something of an oddity; having 1954 Northern Counties lowbridge bodywork and a Leyland Titan OPD2/1 chassis delivered in 1949, it was originally fitted with a single-deck body!

The coach that took us on the tour to these operators on 18 June 1967 was Timpson's 1966 Duple-bodied AEC Reliance JJJ571D, seen here at Hanley.

A very odd vehicle for a BET fleet is Potteries SL996, a 1958 Yeates 'Europa'-bodied Bedford SB8 acquired from Stanier of Newchapel in April 1965. It is seen at Longton on a very wet 24 June 1967 – the following Saturday when I travelled to the Stoke-on-Trent area by train to visit further Potteries' depots!

A **complete** contrast is provided by brand new Alexander-bodied AEC Reliance SL1094 seen out of the rain inside its garage!

A **last** look at Potteries Motor Traction in 1967: 1956 Burlingham-bodied AEC Reliance S677, another acquired from Baxter of Hanley, is seen on their route 7, bound for Longton.

A trip to Merseyside finds Ribble 1958 full-front Burlingham-bodied Leyland Titan PD3/4 No.1531 outside Liverpool, Lime Street station on 1 July 1967.

Back in the Midlands, Trent 1959 dual purpose Willowbrook-bodied Leyland Tiger Cub PSUC1/12 No.152 loads up in Derby Bus Station on 2 July 1967.

Ribble 1954 Saro-bodied Leyland Tiger Cub PSUC1/1 No.410 is seen on a misty morning at Carnforth on 26 August 1967. At this time, I was spending a week in the Lancashire and Cumberland areas photographing the last surviving British Railways steam engines in service.

Similar Ribble Saro-bodied Tiger Cub No.422 stands outside Carnforth Station the same morning.

Earlier Ribble single-decker No.260 stands in their Carlisle garage on 27 August 1967. It is a 44-seat Weymann-bodied Leyland Olympic HR44, dating from 1951 and by now quite a rarity.

Ribble 1958 Burlingham Seagull-bodied Leyland Tiger Cub PSUC1/2 No.1004 is seen in Carlisle Bus Station on 29 August 1967 working route 637 to Penrith.

Sunderland District was a subsidiary of major BET operator Northern General. Here on 30 August 1967, their 1955 Weymann Orion-bodied Leyland Titan PD2/12 No.278 changes crew in Sunderland.

Northern General itself was well-known for being the only operator outside London to buy AEC/Park Royal Routemasters, of which fifty were supplied in 1964/65. One of the earlier batch, No.2094, is also seen in Sunderland that day. The solitary London Transport forward-entrance Routemaster, RMF 1254, which was the prototype for their vehicles, was also acquired by Northern General. After their withdrawal in 1979/80, some of these buses were bought by London Transport, but found not to be suitable for use on London stage-carriage routes. A few, however, did see use as sightseeing buses in the capital with other operators.

A more typical Northern General double-decker is No. 1765, a 63-seat Park Royal-bodied Leyland Titan PD2/12 seen outside Sunderland Station. It was one of a batch of ten delivered in 1957. A United Automobile Service Bristol MW stands behind it.

Their No.1787 is a typical Northern General single-decker, a 44-seat Weymann-bodied Leyland Tiger Cub PSUC1/1 also delivered in 1957, one of a batch of twenty. Another of their Routemasters brings up the rear.

An earlier Leyland Tiger Cub PSUC1/1 single-decker seen in Sunderland that day is Sunderland District No.272, one of thirteen built with Saunders 44-seat bodywork in 1954.

Back in Carlisle on 31 August 1967, Ribble 1958 Burlingham-bodied full-fronted Leyland Titan PD3/4 No.1540 works local route C4.

Down south again, Timpson's 1958 Weymann Fanfare-bodied AEC Reliance VXP 507 stands on a very wet Sunday, 3 September 1967, in one of the coach parks at 'sunny' Clacton. Nothing worse than a day trip to the seaside on a rainy day!

One of North Western's strange-looking Strachan-bodied Bedford VAL14s, No.130 dating from 1964, stands at Warrington Bus Station on 9 September 1967. They were built specifically to enable them to get under a VERY low bridge in Dunham Woodhouses, Cheshire.

On 16 September 1967, Samuelson's touring coach 446 BXD crosses Westminster Bridge working London Transport's Round London Sightseeing Tour. It is an AEC Reliance with Duple Britannia bodywork, new in 1961.

A visit to Oxford on 1 October 1967 finds their 1956 Park Royal lowbridge-bodied exposed radiator AEC Regent V No.183 leaving the city's bus station on a route 67 relief journey. By now, this was one of the oldest double-deckers in the fleet.

This scene in City of Oxford Motor Services' Cowley Road garage provides an interesting comparison between Weymann lowbridge-bodied AEC Regent Vs No.193 & 195 dating from 1957 and Park Royal-bodied example No.185 of the same batch as the one seen above. Once again, all have exposed radiators, which was quite unusual for Regent Vs.

Also in Cowley Road garage on 1 October 1967, 1954 Weymann Orion highbridge-bodied Regent IIIs Nos.937, 941, 940 and 938 have recently been withdrawn and await disposal.

The difference in height between these Weymann-bodied AEC Regent Vs is clearly apparent: 1955-built No.947 is a highbridge version, whilst No.189, dating from 1956, is lowbridge.

Outside the garage is City of Oxford 1963 Marshall-bodied 53-seat AEC Reliance No.773, one of several 36ft-long single-deckers of this style in their fleet.

On this occasion, I travelled to the town of Witney aboard 1960 Weymann-bodied 44-seater AEC Reliance No.747 which is seen at City of Oxford's route 54 terminus in the town's High Street.

My purpose in travelling to the town was to visit the City of Oxford garage there, in which AEC Reliance No.738, now due for early withdrawal is seen. It carries Willowbrook 43-seat bodywork and dates from 1955. Park Royal-bodied AEC Bridgemaster No.315 noses in on the right and was built in 1961.

Back in Oxford Bus Station, 1956 Weymann lowbridge-bodied AEC Regent V No.192 has been at work on route 6.

Also there is Stratford Blue 1962 Marshall dual-purpose 41-seater Leyland Tiger Cub PSUC1/1 No.51, working route 14 to its home town. In addition to the two BET fleets seen here, Tilling Group fleets Thames Valley and United Counties also worked stage carriage services to this bus station.

Autumn leaves
begin to fall as 1961
City of Oxford AEC
Reliance No.760
lays over at the bus
station after duty
on route 57. It has
Marshall 44-seat
bodywork.

BET operator
Yorkshire Woollen
District served the
city of Bradford,
where their 1961
Northern Counties-
bodied 80-seat
forward entrance AEC
Regent V No.847 has
terminated on route
67 from Huddersfield
on 7 October
1967. Possibly
the illuminated
advertisement panel
relieves the Regent's
otherwise drab all-
red livery!

A trip to Birmingham on 15 October 1967 finds Midland Red S14 single-decker No. 4553 outside their Digbeth garage. Built in 1957, it is of their own manufacture.

Inside the garage, elderly Midland Red-built C2 touring coach No.3350, new in 1950, has recently received this smart new Plaxton body.

On a snowy 9 January 1968, Samuelson's 1961 Duple Britannia-bodied AEC Reliance 443 BXD awaits departure from Victoria, Buckingham Palace Road, on London Transport's Round London Sightseeing Tour. Note the LT 'bullseye' reading 'Round Tour' on the wall on the right.

Back to Wembley again! The occasion is the Schoolboys' International football match, for which Southdown subsidiary Triumph of Southsea 1958 Beadle-bodied Leyland Tiger Cub PSUC1/2 coach T1126 arrives. Coincidentally, this operator's light blue and cream livery was of the same colours as the labels of Joe Meek's Triumph label independent records of 1960 – or perhaps it was not a coincidence!

I was at Wembley again the following week, on 9 March 1968, for another sporting event. Another BET subsidiary fleet was Skinner's Coaches of Hastings, which as we saw earlier came under Maidstone & District. This is their 1961 Harrington Wayfarer-bodied AEC Reliance C443.

An older Maidstone & District coach at Wembley that day is 1954 Harrington-bodied AEC Reliance C316, now due for early withdrawal.

Also dating from 1954, KCY 488 is a rare Guy Arab LUF with Park Royal 41-seat bodywork belonging to one of the smallest BET companies, Neath & Cardiff Luxury Coaches who operated coaches only in the Cardiff, Neath and Swansea areas.

An unusual visitor to the London area on 10 March 1968, seen near Heathrow Airport, is this Mexborough & Swinton 1953 Duple-bodied Leyland Royal Tiger, recently acquired from Southdown.

Freshly painted for the 1968 summer season, East Kent wartime Guy Arab I BJG 461 is one of two which have come up to London for the Epsom Derby on 29 May 1968, seen after depositing its passengers at Victoria Coach Station that evening.

An OTC trip to South Yorkshire on 16 June 1968 finds Yorkshire Traction No.770 at their Barnsley depot. Things are not quite what they seem with this Leyland, since it started life as a Tiger PS1 single-decker, but was rebodied with a new Roe 59-seat double-deck body in 1957, and also reregistered.

Also at Barnsley, No.460 is a Leyland Tiger Cub PSUC1/1 with Park Royal 44-seat bodywork, new in 1958.

Yorkshire Traction No.427 is also a 44-seat Tiger Cub PSUC1/1, but has Willowbrook bodywork and was new in 1957.

Looking very smart, No.502 is a Tiger Cub PSUC1/12 new in 1962 with the style of Alexander bodywork usually seen on coaches, though it is a 45-seat bus.

Seen in Barnsley Bus Station, Yorkshire Traction No.699 is a Leyland Titan PD2/12 with Northern Counties 55-seat lowbridge bodywork. It was new in 1953.

Also at the bus station is No.440, another of the Park Royal-bodied Leyland Tiger Cub PSUC1/1s, new in 1958.

One of Yorkshire Traction's coaches is No.114, one of six Leyland Tiger Cub PSUC1/1s with Burlingham Seagull 70 41-seat bodies new in 1961.

Yorkshire Traction
No.779 is another Leyland Tiger PS1 rebodied as a double-decker by Roe in 1957. There were twelve of these so treated.

No.690 is by now one of the oldest vehicles in Yorkshire Traction's fleet, being a 55-seat lowbridge all-Leyland Titan PD2/12, new in 1952.

Seen outside Western Welsh's Barry depot on 22 September 1968, No.1272 is a dual-purpose Metro-Cammell-bodied Leyland Tiger Cub PSUC1/2 41-seater new in 1960.

Four days later, on 26 September 1968, another Western Welsh single-decker is on show at the Earls Court Commercial Motor Show. No.1399 is a Leyland Tiger Cub PSUC1/12 with Marshall 43-seat bodywork.

On a wintry 29 March 1969, Southdown still had some traditional half-cab double-deckers running on routes in Brighton which were pooled with Brighton Corporation and Brighton, Hove & District. The latter operator had in fact recently been taken over by Southdown following the BET group's purchase by the Transport Holding Company Ltd. as a prelude to the formation of the National Bus Company. No.785, a 1956 Beadle-bodied Leyland Titan PD2/12, heads north from Old Steine on route 38.

Another Southdown Leyland Titan PD2/12 dating from 1956, No.811 has East Lancs bodywork and is seen in Preston Road working the long 119 route from Tunbridge Wells which was jointly operated with Maidstone & District. Note the platform doors on this vehicle, which is very well filled!

For the 1969 season, a number of East Kent's 1951 Park Royal-bodied Guy Arab IIIs were converted to open-toppers, finally replacing the wartime utility Arabs. FFN 377 is one of two up in London on Derby Day, 4 June 1969, and is seen here passing Putney Station. Three years later, buses of this batch were loaned to London Transport for their Round London Sightseeing Tour.